KIDS THROUGHOUT HISTORY™

Kids During the Age of Exploration

Cynthia MacGregor

The Rosen Publishing Group's
PowerKids Press™
New York

Published in 1999 by The Rosen Publishing Group, Inc.
29 East 21st Street, New York, NY 10010

First Edition

Book Design: Danielle Primiceri

Photo Credits: Cover © Art Resource; pp. 4, 8, 15 © The Bettmann Archive; p. 7 © Corbis-Bettmann, © Art Resource (inset); pp. 11, 16 © Corbis-Bettmann; p. 12 © Archive Photos; pp. 19, 20 © Giraudon/Art Resource.

MacGregor, Cynthia.
    Kids during the age of exploration / Cynthia MacGregor.
        p.   cm.— (Kids throughout history)
    Includes index.
    Summary: Describes the social and economic climate of the sixteenth century by focusing on the life of an apprentice to a mapmaker living in Spain during the age of exploration.
    ISBN 0-8239-5257-6
    1. Spain—Social life and customs—16th century—Juvenile literature. 2. Children—Spain—History—16th century—Juvenile literature. 3. America—Discovery and exploration—Spanish—Juvenile literature. [1. Spain—Social life and customs—16th century. 2. Spain—History—16th century. 3. America—Discovery and exploration—Spanish.] I. Title. II. Series.
DP171.5.M33 1998
946'.04'—dc21
                                           98-2612
                                               CIP
                                             AC

Manufactured in the United States of America

Contents

Old World/New World

Spain in the year 1550 was an important place in the age of **exploration** (EK-splor-AY-shun). Along with its **rival** (RY-vul), Portugal, Spain was one of the most active countries in exploring the New World of North and South America. **Explorers** (ek-SPLOR-erz) searched for trade **routes** (ROOTS) and new lands. Christopher Columbus was just one of many explorers of the New World. Other explorers made important discoveries too. From the Americas, they brought what they knew of new **cultures** (KUL-cherz) back to Europe.

◄ *Many people consider the first journey of Christopher Columbus to the Americas in 1492 to be the start of the age of exploration.*

Miguel

Miguel felt very lucky to be living in Cadiz in 1550. Cadiz was a busy, seaport city in Spain. Explorers' ships set sail from there. Miguel was twelve and lived with his brother, Juan, his sister, Flor, and their parents. His father **imported** (im-POR-ted) silk from China. His mother took care of Miguel and his brother and sister. Only very poor women had jobs at that time. Miguel's family wasn't rich or poor. They were part of Cadiz's growing middle class.

Kids who lived in port cities were able to watch ships returning from long journeys and see the new things ▶ *explorers brought with them.*

A Kid's Life in Cadiz

Miguel worked as an **apprentice** (uh-PREN-tis) to a mapmaker. Maps were changed often as explorers traveled to new places. Miguel's brother was an apprentice too. He worked for a shipbuilder and was learning to build big ships. Miguel's sister would soon enter a **convent** (KON-vent) to become a nun. Like Miguel and his brother and sister, most kids didn't go to school. But wealthy families had someone come to their homes to teach their children.

Maps, such as this one from 1529, changed with each explorer's new discoveries. This kept mapmakers very busy.

The Ships

Miguel's older cousin, Vicente, had sailed on a few **voyages** (VOY-ih-jez) to America. Miguel asked Vicente about the ships that were used. Ships called **caravels** (KAR-uh-velz) were used by many explorers in the 1400s. They were powered by the ocean winds blowing their sails. In the 1500s, **carracks** (KAR-uks) became popular. They were also powered by wind but were rounder and heavier than the caravels. Carracks were also better able to sail through strong ocean storms. Vicente sailed on carracks.

Ships needed to be very sturdy to travel across the ocean for months at a time. ▶

Trade

Explorers made trips to the Americas after the voyages of Columbus. Trade with the people who lived in the New World was an important part of those trips. Explorers traded glass beads, fishhooks, brass bracelets, silk, wool, and cotton. Native Americans, or people already living in North and South America, traded jewels, gold and silver, spices, foods, and animal skins with the explorers. These things were brought back to Cadiz and other cities in Europe. Europe was part of the Old World as were Africa and Asia.

◀ *Trade helped Native Americans and explorers to understand each other even though they spoke different languages.*

New Maps, New Tastes

All these explorations kept Miguel busy in his work for the mapmaker. As explorers learned of more and more places in the New World, mapmakers had to keep making new maps. Miguel worked hard, but he did learn a lot about **geography** (jee-AH-gruh-fee). As the maps changed, so did the food that Miguel's mother served for dinner. Things from the New World like cocoa, tomatoes, potatoes, spices, and vanilla became popular in kitchens across Europe. Miguel's favorite food from the New World was sweet corn.

Native Americans introduced the explorers to many different foods. These foods soon made their way ▶ onto dinner tables in the Old World.

Animals

Vicente also told Miguel about animals he had seen in the New World. At first, these creatures sounded so strange that Miguel thought Vicente was making them up. Vicente told Miguel about seeing bears, pumas, opossums, and turkeys. He talked about different kinds of deer and beautiful birds, such as eagles. These animals were unheard of in the Old World! Explorers also brought animals, like horses, to the New World. Before they did, there had not been any horses in the Americas.

◀ *Before arriving in the Americas, explorers had never seen a North American black bear.*

Homes

Miguel's family lived in a small house with a dirt floor. The bedrooms were cold and dark. All the window openings built into their house were covered with paper because glass was very expensive. But not everyone in Cadiz lived like Miguel. One day Miguel's boss sent him to deliver a map to a wealthy man. His house was beautiful and much bigger than Miguel's. The walls had pretty tiles all over them. There were lots of glass windows which made the man's home sunny and bright.

Seaport cities, like Cadiz in Spain and Lisbon in Portugal, were crowded because there were usually more jobs there than in the country. ▶

Hard Times

In 1530 a tenth of the people in Cadiz were poor. By 1560 almost a quarter of Cadiz's people had become poor. During that time, landowners began trading with **settlers** (SET-ul-erz) and Native Americans in the New World instead of farming. The landowners earned more money through trade and some shut down their farms. This left the people of Cadiz who worked on these farms poor and without jobs. Many moved to the Americas where they hoped to find better jobs and better lives.

◀ *Kids in Cadiz, like this young boy, watched explorers leave for long journeys. They dreamed of being able to see the New World too.*

A New Life

As Miguel grew older and worked on his maps, he began to wonder if it was time to leave Cadiz. He wished he could see the places that he drew, like many of his friends had. But Miguel didn't want to be a sailor, or a **missionary** (MISH-un-eh-ree) as many of them were. After all, he knew so much about mapmaking. Luckily, Vicente helped Miguel get a job as a mapmaker on an explorer's ship leaving from Cadiz. It was the first of many exciting journeys to the New World for Miguel.

Glossary

apprentice (uh-PREN-tis) A young person learning a skill or a trade.

caravel (KAR-uh-vel) A ship used in the 1400s that was powered by sails.

carrack (KAR-uk) A ship used in the 1500s that was powered by sails.

convent (KON-vent) A group of nuns living together who teach religion and care for poor and sick people.

culture (KUL-cher) The beliefs, customs, art, and religions of a group of people.

exploration (EK-splor-AY-shun) When someone travels to new lands for adventure or discovery.

explorer (ek-SPLOR-er) A person who travels to different places to learn more about those lands.

geography (jee-AH-gruh-fee) The study of the earth's surface.

import (IM-port) To bring in from another country.

missionary (MISH-un-eh-ree) A person who teaches a religion to the people of another country or people with different beliefs.

rival (RY-vul) Someone who tries to beat someone else at something.

route (ROOT) The path you take to get somewhere.

settler (SET-ul-er) A person who moves to a new land to live.

voyage (VOY-ij) A journey by water.

Index